lonely planet kids

ARE YOU READY FOR AN ADVENTURE

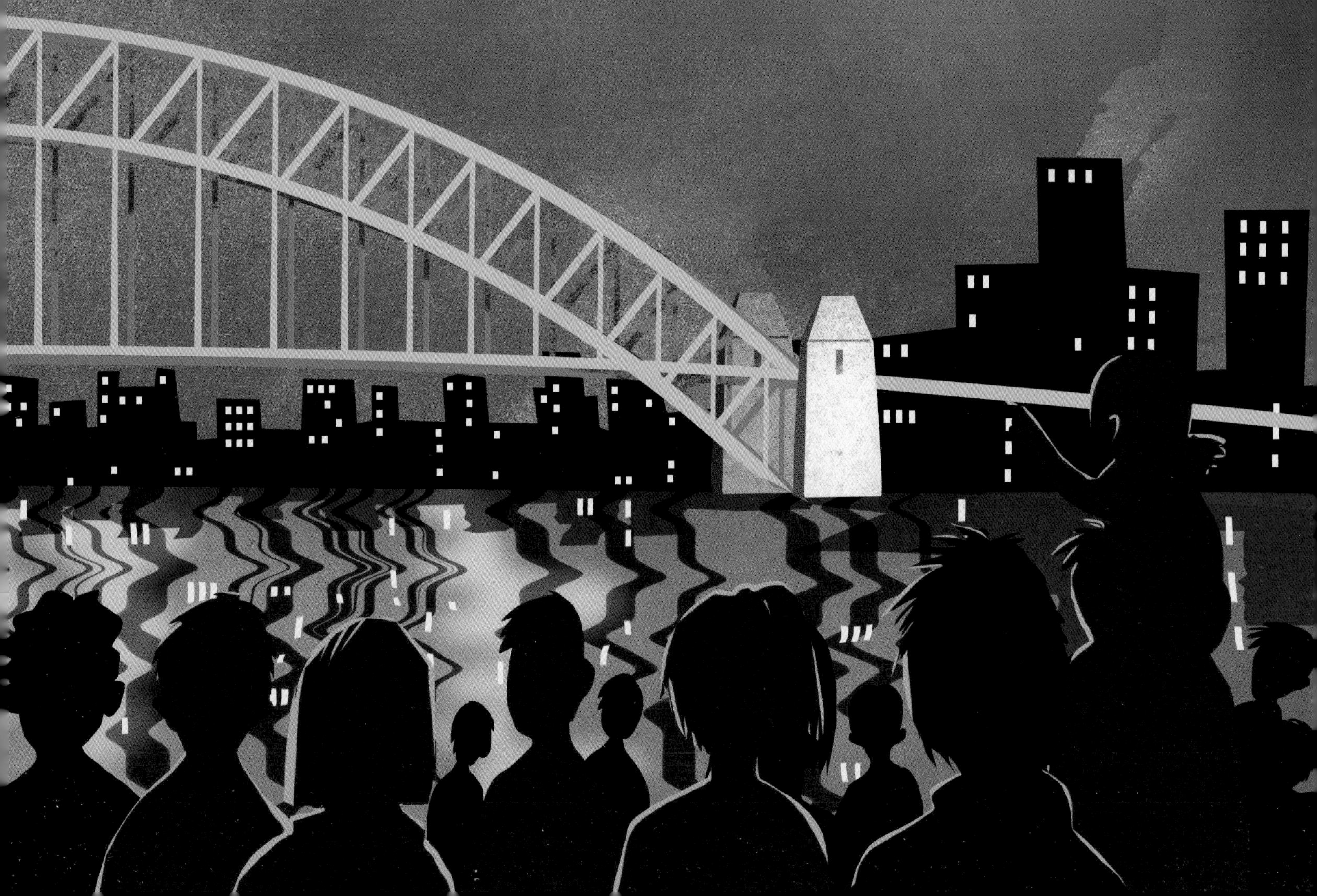

ACKNOWLEDGMENTS

Publishing Director	Piers Pickard
Publisher	Tim Cook
Commissioning Editor	Jen Feroze
Authors	Jen Feroze, Christina Webb
Assistant Editor	Christina Webb
Illustrators	Cherie Zamazing
	David Shephard
	Mike Love
Designer	Andy Mansfield
Print production	Larissa Frost, Nigel Longuet

Thanks to: Jennifer Dixon

Published in February 2017 by Lonely Planet Global Ltd
CRN: 554153
ISBN: 978 1 78657 230 1
www.lonelyplanetkids.com
© Lonely Planet 2016
Printed in Malaysia

10 9 8 7 6 5 4 3 2 1

Lonely Planet Offices

AUSTRALIA
The Malt Store, Level 3, 551 Swanston St,
Carlton, Victoria 3053
T: 03 8379 8000

IRELAND
Unit E, Digital Court, The Digital Hub,
Rainsford St, Dublin 8

USA
124 Linden St, Oakland, CA 94607
T: 510 250 6400

UK
240 Blackfriars Rd, London, SE1 8NW
T: 020 3771 5100

STAY IN TOUCH lonelyplanet.com/contact

LET'S EXPLORE
CITY

Cherie Zamazing,
David Shephard, and Mike Love

Are you ready for an adventure?
Two explorers, Marco and Amelia, are off to see the bright lights of the world's big cities, and they've invited you to come, too!

The best explorers need to be ready for anything. Look at the list below and add stickers to the next page to get ready to go. Check the items off the list when you've stuck them on.

City Explorers' Gear

MARCO

- Sneakers
- Jeans
- Shirt
- Backpack
- Camera
- Map

AMELIA

- Sneakers
- Pants
- Long-sleeved T-shirt
- Tablet
- Backpack

Times Square in New York City comes alive at night in a crazy jumble of bright neon signs. Use your sharpest spotting skills to find a pair of identical adverts.

This famous statue was a gift to New York from France in 1886.
Connect the dots to reveal the city's most famous lady.

Brrr! Marco and Amelia are visiting the Canadian city of Montreal, where snow has turned the Parc du Mont-Royal into a winter wonderland.

Add more snow-tubers, sledders, and skaters to
the snowy scene with your stickers.

Marco and Amelia have landed in Los Angeles. They're feeling a little starstruck on Hollywood Boulevard, where you can find celebrity handprints and stars along the Walk of Fame. See if you can spot the items listed below in the busy scene.

Can you find...
5 stars
3 pairs of handprints
1 superhero
2 unicycles
4 cameras

Thousands of seals splash around off the coast of Cape Town in South Africa! Marco and Amelia are daytripping from the city to Seal Island to spot as many of the friendly creatures as they can. Can you help them count how many seals there are in this scene?

No visit to Bangkok, Thailand, would be complete without a trip to one of the famous floating markets nearby. Marco and Amelia have come to Damnoen Saduak — one of the most famous.

Boats are filled with piles of exotic fruit, vegetables, coconuts, and pots of hot noodle and rice dishes to sell. Add stickers to make the bustling market scene extra delicious!

Queenstown in New Zealand is known as the adventure capital of the world, and with good reason. From bungee jumping to skydiving to white-water rafting — it's got it all!

Can you spot all eight differences between these two sky-high scenes over the city?

Ooooh! Aaaaaah! The New Year's Eve fireworks over Sydney Harbour are some of the best in the world. They light up the bridge and the famous Opera House.

Use your stickers to fill the sky with fireworks, and help Marco and Amelia start the new year in style.

Our two explorers have touched down in Dhaka, Bangladesh, and it's really busy! There are over 400,000 rickshaws riding around the city streets every day. Can you help Marco and Amelia through the maze of rickshaws and get them across the street safely?

START

Hong Kong has more skyscrapers than any other city in the world! Marco and Amelia are in the harbor on a traditional Chinese ship called a 'junk', gazing at the thousands of bright lights at dusk.

Use your stickers to complete the sparkling Hong Kong skyline.

Marco and Amelia are on Jingu Bashi bridge in Tokyo — a great place to see people dressed in a cool and colorful style known as "Harajuku."

Add stickers to complete the fantastical fashions and make everything super *kawaii* (the Japanese word for "cute"!).

Dubai is a city with no limits. It's broken countless world records!
Let's have a look at some of the city's greatest achievements.

World's tallest building

The Burj Khalifa

World's longest handmade chain

It was over 3 miles (5 km) long!

World's largest same-name gathering

1,096 people all called Mohammed!

Amelia and Marco are in Moscow, Russia, looking at St. Basil's Cathedral — one of the world's most colorful buildings. The huge domes were designed to look like flames rising into the sky. Wow!

Use markers to color the cathedral and other buildings in Moscow's Red Square.

Venice at carnival time is a magical place. The streets and canals are filled with people in beautiful gowns, masks, and headdresses.

Use markers to design your own marvelous mask here.

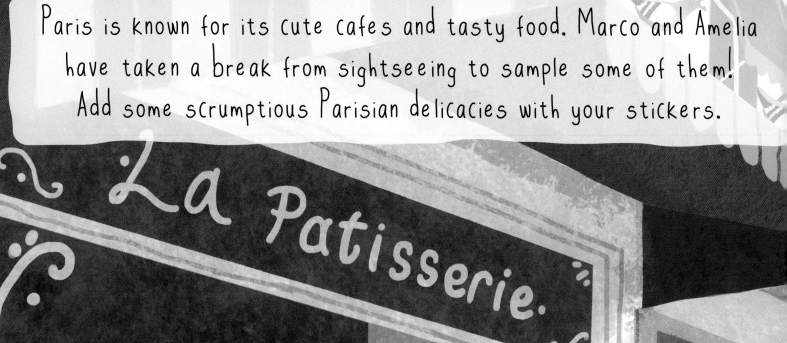

Paris is known for its cute cafes and tasty food. Marco and Amelia have taken a break from sightseeing to sample some of them! Add some scrumptious Parisian delicacies with your stickers.

La Patisserie.

One of the best ways to get around London is to catch one of the city's famous red double-decker buses! Follow these steps to draw your own London bus.

1 First, draw the basic outline shown here in pencil. Don't worry about the wheels just yet.

2 Next, draw the two large front windows and two door shapes on the side.

3 Add the rest of the windows along the side of the bus.

4 Now add the side-view mirror, lights, destination sign, and wheels, then extra lines on the doors and windows. Finally, go over it in pen and erase the pencil.

LONDON

It's busy on Westminster Bridge near Big Ben! Finish the big red bus we've started here for you.

Parts of Buenos Aires in Argentina are covered with incredible street art. Artists use the walls and buildings to express themselves or tell important stories about the country's past.

Using markers, create your own piece of street art on this blank wall. What story will you tell?

Havana in Cuba is the largest city in the Caribbean. It's known for its pastel-perfect old buildings and matching classic cars.

Complete the colorful scene with your stickers!

The world's cities contain some amazing landmarks — from buildings full of history to shiny modern skyscrapers. Read the facts below, and see if you can match each one with the correct landmark.

A

EIFFEL TOWER

1. This beautiful building's name means "Crown of Palaces." It's made of marble and took 22 years to complete.

BURJ KHALIFA

B

2. This structure is painted in a color called "International Orange," and is often covered in thick fog.

GOLDEN GATE BRIDGE

C

3. A man named Jørn Utzon designed this unique building. He won US$8,000 in a competition for his design!

D

TAJ MAHAL

4. Kings and queens have been imprisoned here, and some have even had their heads chopped off!

TOWER OF LONDON

E

5. This gleaming tower is the tallest building in the world. It has a whopping 163 floors.

SYDNEY OPERA HOUSE

F

6. When this landmark was first built, people nicknamed it the "metal asparagus"!

Our explorers are in Mexico City attending the Day of the Dead festival — an event that celebrates the lives of loved ones who have passed away. There's face-painting, flowers, and lots of food!

Finish the colorful scene with your stickers.

Soccer is the world's most popular sport, and it has the biggest following in South America. Amelia and Marco are kicking a ball around with the local mascots at the Maracanã Stadium in Rio de Janeiro.

The mascot Biriba is based on a stray dog who used to visit the stadium, and the Admiral mascot is a Portuguese sea captain.

Be inspired by these Brazilian team mascots and create your own sporting buddy to join the game!

Can you find these items from your city adventure hidden in the grid below?

FESTIVAL

LIGHTS

MARKET

STATUE

SKYSCRAPER

TAXI

STADIUM

S A I D U T K L M X R J
T K W O F E S T I V A L
A T Y X E U D J O V S K
T K V S D M K A I M T O
U G O E C A I O E L A A
E I A M H R L S R I D S
O G O F A K A X O C I M
I F H E X E V P S H U I
G X I S I T S O E Z M S
E M A R L P A M I R C X
T D K T F C D O V K E Y
Q O E S V L I G H T S A

Marco and Amelia have had
an amazing time exploring the
cities of the world, but now
it's time to head back home.
Will you join them on their
next adventure?

Answers

Check all your answers here... but no cheating!

Matching Ads

Dot To Dot

It's the Statue of Liberty!

Walk Of Fame Game

Counting Seals

There are 45 seals!

Spot The Difference

Rickshaw Route

City Landmarks

1. D   4. E
2. C   5. B
3. F   6. A

Word Search